MW00635999

THE HISTORY OF CURLING

A CONCISE ESSAY ON THIS POPULAR WINTER SPORT
INCLUDING ITS HISTORY, PRINCIPLES AND RULES.

—

BY

BERTRAM SMITH

—

British Library Cataloguing-in-Publication Data
A catalogue record for this book is available from
the British Library

CONTENTS

—

CURLING

I

A NATIONAL GAME

IN its antiquity, dignity, and universal grip upon the
hearts of the people of Scotland curling holds a position of its own among national games. There is no
other so broadly and so genuinely national as this, no
other which bulks so largely in the life of the people
as a whole. Curling was created by the people, and
has always belonged—in Scotland at least—absolutely to the people. It has never been developed
into a scientific exhibition for the benefit of spectators.
It has never been invaded by professionalism, and
the interest that it calls forth does not depend upon
seeing it played, or reading newspaper reports. It
rests upon the village clubs, the parish matches, and
the great bonspiels, which are not made up of picked
champions of a county or district, but of the rank
and file of players representative of almost every
parish.

There has been a vast development of curling in
the last fifty years in England, Canada, Switzerland,
New Zealand, and elsewhere, and in these new homes,
and under new conditions its character has often
undergone a change, but in Scotland curling is still,
as it has always been, the game of the working man,

CURLING

There are many reasons why it should be so. It is, in the first place, exceedingly cheap and simple. The player requires nothing but his stones, which he probably inherits from his father—curling stones seldom break, and never wear out—and a broom, which he can generally find behind the door, or cut for himself from the hillside. His club subscription may be anything from one shilling to half a crown. And all that remains is to gather eight players together and find a sheet of water fifty yards in length. There are few Scottish parishes without a pond or lake of some sort. Then again he need not neglect his work to play. A hard frost in the country districts puts a stop to nearly all outdoor work. Ploughing, draining, dyking, and building in all its forms are suspended, and farmers are able to find time for all that they have to do in this dead season during the morning or evening, and to take three hours in the middle of the day for their game. There are no doubt many—carpenters, blacksmiths and others—who have no good reason for leaving their work, but they are also engulfed in the wave of enthusiasm which comes with the fall in the thermometer. Curling is an institution and a tradition. A spell of frost is at the best a rare event, and employers as well as labourers are generally willing to make the most of the ice when it is there, and try to overtake neglected duties when the thaw comes. The secretary of the curling club for the time being rules the parish with an absolute authority.

Thus it is that curling has spread and prospered, and the Annual of the Royal Caledonian Club—which is to curling what the M.C.C. is to cricket—has grown year by year in size and interest, till it is a volume of surprising proportions. It now contains lists of members of nearly seven hundred affiliated clubs in

Scotland, and as there are many clubs not included and there must be many players who are not actually members of a club, it is probably safe to estimate the number of curlers in Scotland at between forty and fifty thousand. But in dealing with figures of Scottish curling everything is on a grand scale. One does not reckon with teams, but with battalions. A bonspiel is not the meeting of two rival elevens or fifteens, it is the assembling of an army. When the North meets the South in the " Grand Match " at Carsbreck there are over two thousand players on the ice, and there are many other minor engagements, which count their curlers by the hundred, or even by the thousand. Indeed, so long as both sides can bring forward an equal tally of rinks there need be no limit to the numbers taking part in a bonspiel, as the whole of the scores are massed together at the close, and the side with the majority wins. The cup is then allotted to the club on the winning side having the largest average of shots " up "—that is after deducting their opponents' scores—and goes finally to the skip in that club, whose rink has the largest majority.

Such is the game in Scotland—the ruling passion in the lives of thousands of working men, and eagerly adopted by many who are in a better position to pick and choose their pastimes. But the game no longer belongs to Scotland alone. It has spread in the last century far and wide, and has found a footing whereever ice exists and a few Scotchmen have been able to come together and form the nucleus of a club.

At home the curler is labouring always under severe disadvantages. He is completely dependent upon the freaks of a miserable climate. There are seasons when he cannot play at all ; and ice is such a variable factor that many great matches must be played in a thaw and under wretched conditions.

At the best he gets perhaps a week or two of decent ice in the year, and dare never look more than a day ahead with any confidence, while there is no season without its list of broken engagements and unfinished games. He must often cast longing eyes to Switzerland and to Canada, where the game is played daily under ideal conditions and on glorious ice. It has been developed there to an infinitely delicate science far beyond what is possible on the rough Scotch rinks. There are now many strong clubs in Switzerland, where the game was introduced about the year 1870, and in the leading Alpine resorts it may be seen any day throughout the winter season. The players are almost entirely Anglo-Swiss, and the artificial rinks on which they play usually belong to the leading hotels. The native Swiss have not yet seriously taken up the game, probably because ice in a land where everything is smothered beneath feet of snow is a highly expensive luxury.

But by far the greatest curling country is Canada, and the curling capital of Canada, and therefore of the world, is Winnipeg.

There is one little peculiarity of the game of curling, one among many points in which it is unique. It is, so far as I know, the only great outdoor game that is played without a ball.

II

A GAME OF LONG AGO

THERE have been many heated controversies as to the origin of curling. Though much close and brilliant argument has been brought forward in support of each of the two favourite theories, I do not know that any absolute conclusion has been established. It is, however, quite safe to say that the game was either invented centuries ago in Scotland, or that its origin was Flemish, and it was introduced at an early date into Scotland. The Flemish theory is based upon the derivation of many of the terms and expressions in use. It does not seem to me a matter of very great importance whether the first germ of the game is Scotch or Flemish, but in the latter case one is inclined to remark that its inventors did not know a good thing when they had it, for in a very short time the game was completely annexed by Scotland, and has belonged to Scotland ever since. At any rate, it is quite certain that curling has been practised for fully three centuries, and has slowly and by natural stages developed from a rough and tumble sport to a great game of skill. The stones were at first mere boulders gathered out of some mountain burn, irregular and unshaped. It is most interesting to trace the slow changes and improvements that came with the years. At first the under side is rubbed smooth, so that the stone may glide upon the ice and need not be thrown bouncing and turning on its rough surfaces. Later, one finds the first attempt at shaping a handle by means of holes cut for the thumb and forefinger. All this time the stones are becoming more and more circular in shape till the day of the round stone with a fixed iron handle arrives. From this it is only a short step to the final development of a movable handle and a stone with two soles (so that it can be played on either side) and to all the finer points of polish and of " cups " which are now in practice. The curling-stone as it is turned out to-day by the best manufacturers is a beautiful and finished product, but the material is still in many cases the same. There is no stone more popular than that which is known as a " Burnock Water," made from the boulders found in the heart of the stream, and to many Scots a curling-stone is still a " Channel-stane."

It was the custom in the old days to play eight men a side, each armed with one stone, generally of huge proportions. The regulations limiting the size and weight of stones did not come into force till well on in the nineteenth century, and before that the game must have been in a great measure a test of strength and endurance as well as skill, for some of the old historic stones still in existence are 70 or 80 pounds in weight. These were often by a pleasant conceit named after mountains, such as " Queensberry " and " Criffel." One can picture to oneself the Homeric battles of old with eight giants labouring upon either side. One can well imagine that when the thaw set in the weaker brethren would fall short one by one, and sheer brute strength at the last would carry the day. For it must have been of little use to oppose these vast engines of war with anything of smaller mettle. It would not be easy with a modern stone, if the ice were dull, to make any impression upon masses of granite such as these, and a shot sitting securely on the tee would "take some shifting," as the saying goes.

It is a far cry from that strange, barbaric game of old to the precise and dainty "drawing-room curling" of, let us say, a ladies' club in Switzerland. But what the game has lost in grandeur it has gained in grace, and though we may now need less strength to excel in it, there is far greater scope for finer qualities, of head and hand and eye.

And so Scotland played on for a long tale of years —there are clubs still existing which have flourished continuously for over two centuries—and visitors from other lands, when by chance they came upon a game in progress, looked on in amazement as at some savage orgy beyond the understanding of civilised man. Curling to the Englishman was a standing joke. But at last, in the nineteenth century, it began to spread over the globe and take its place among the great games of skill. A curling club was formed in Montreal in the year 1807, and the first game in Toronto was played upon the frozen surface of the bay in 1840. As soon as the conquest of Canada was complete the game was carried over the frontier into the United States. There are now several flourishing clubs in Chicago, Buffalo, and New York. The development in Switzerland is a matter of more recent history, but the game is now making steady progress there, and has a great future before it. There are a dozen clubs in New Zealand. Finally, we find in the "Royal Annual" the name of a Russian club with its headquarters in Moscow, so that curling may be said to reach from the far East, to what one might well suppose to be the western limit of civilisation, judging by such names as Neepewa and Wawanesa, which also occur in its pages.

Curling is, of course, very popular in the Northern counties of England.

III

THE PRINCIPLES OF CURLING

THOSE who have never seen the game of curling played can best form an idea of it by studying the points in which it resembles, and those in which it differs from, the familiar game of bowls. The rinks are made up of four men a side, each of whom delivers two stones at each " head " or " end." These are the lead, the second man, the back-hand, and the last player who is generally the skip. The skip is in supreme command of his force and directs the game throughout, showing each player exactly where he wishes him to play his stone, and instructing the two sweepers as to how far it is to be brought. The "tee" at which one plays is not, as in bowls, a movable quantity. It is simply a small round hole cut in the ice. This is the centre of the " house "—a seven-foot circle, marked upon the surface of the ice. There are two smaller circles, or rings, inside of this, all three having their centre at the tee. The rings have no special significance beyond showing clearly how the stones are lying, but no stone which is not in or touching the house can score. The scoring is other-wise the same as in bowls ; that is to say, that at the conclusion of a head the side having a stone nearest to the tee scores one for each shot that is better than the best of its opponents. At a distance of seven yards from the tee a line is drawn across the rink—the "hog," or "hog-score"—and any stone failing to reach this line is taken off the ice. The house is marked out at each end of the rink, and the heads are played alternately up and down. It is thirty-eight yards from the foot-score—where the stone is delivered —to the tee.

As the game proceeds the four men composing the rink are all fully occupied. The skip stands in the house, directing operations. One player is delivering his stone, and the other two are sweeping. "Sweeping" consists in polishing the surface of the ice before the running stone, by plying a broom back and forth, very much as one would brush a floor. The side to which the running stone belongs may sweep in this way before it if it is delivered with too little force; and the moment that it has passed the tee the opposing skip may sweep it out of the house in the same manner. When it is the skip's turn to play, he hands over the control of affairs to another member of the rink, probably his back-hand man, who is then in absolute charge of the head.

There are two methods of forming a stand, or, as a golfer would say, a "stance," for the player. He must, as will readily be understood, have a good footing upon the ice to swing and deliver his stone. For this purpose he plays either from a "hack" (or "stell") or from a "crampit." The crampit is an iron plate about three feet long, laid upon or frozen into the ice. The hack is simply a nick cut in the ice large enough for the sole of the right foot to rest against the incision. There is much controversy as to which is the better method. Both are admitted by the rules, and hack players despise the crampit quite as heartily as crampit players detest the hack. Opinion is divided in Scotland. Switzerland favours the crampit. Canada uses nothing but the hack, which is often there formed by freezing a small block of wood on the surface of the ice. There is at least this much to be said for the crampit men; that on lake ice of moderate thickness the cutting of the hack sometimes brings up the water and spoils the " Board."

Another point in dispute is the "dolly," which is much used in some parts of Scotland, and entirely ignored in others, and which has been universally adopted in Switzerland. This is simply a wooden ninepin, which stands on the tee. It is so light in comparison with the stones, that it does not in any way affect the game, as the slightest touch knocks it out of the house, and its object is simply to show the player, at the moment of playing, where the tee is. It must be remembered that the player is nearly forty yards away, and can often see nothing but a confused bunch of stones. Many of the old school of Scotch curlers strongly object to the use of the dolly. And I have every sympathy with their contention. Their idea it is that it distracts the player to have two objects to consider ; that it is no affair of his where the tee may be ; it is his duty to play for the skip's broom. But it seems that on the whole the dolly is gaining ground. The spectators like it, as it makes it easier for them to follow the play, but curling is not a game for spectators.

The size of curling stones is limited by the rules to a circumference of 36 inches, and the weight to 44 lb. The usual weight is between 38 and 42 lb. They are made of granite or river boulders, cut with a sole on each side, and beautifully polished. The chief makes now in use are Ailsas, Crawford Johns, and Burnock Waters. The first-mentioned is a beautiful granite stone, blue or grey. Crawford Johns are of a sort of plum-pudding black and grey, and Burnock Waters are almost black. Ailsas are the favourite stones in Switzerland. In Canada iron stones are in almost universal use. They are found to be better suited to the hard ice of that severe climate. The two sides of a stone are differently cut, so that one side is keener and runs more easily than the other. Thus when the ice is heavy one can turn a stone from the "dour" (or "drug") side to the "keen" side. This may be done during a game.

IV

THE ART OF CURLING

THE player on taking up his position on the crampit should first carefully clean the sole of his stone. He then assumes an easy posture, with his right foot at right angles to the line of play, and his left about a yard in advance, with its toe pointing straight down the rink. He lays his stone down well in front of him, near his left foot, and looks up for directions. In Scotch curling, where a good deal of force is often used, much depends upon the swing with which the stone is delivered. The weight is thrown on the right foot, and the player swings freely and easily with the whole body, bringing the stone well back. It is a very bad fault to swing stiffly with the arm alone, and it is absolutely essential to swing straight, and not— as most beginners do—to "pull" the stone round behind the right leg. Finally the stone must, however strongly the shot is played, reach the ice smoothly at the moment that it leaves the hand, and glide straight away on an even bottom.

In Switzerland and Canada swing is a matter of very small account. The ice is so keen that it is only necessary to lift the stone a few inches and lay it gently down. But even under these conditions there must be no trace of stiffness in the action. From the moment that he lifts his stone to play the player must keep his eye fixed upon the skip's broom, which is

OUT-HANDLE.

IN-HANDLE.

13

directing the shot. Although that is a very elementary instruction, many beginners—they may for all I know be golfers, who have been told to "keep their eye on the ball"—are apt to look down in the course of the swing, which is fatal. The player must always remember that it is his duty simply to play the shot that is put before him. He need have no theories as to what is the best shot to play under the circumstances, for that is a matter which rests entirely with the skip. He will be asked for a stone played on a certain line with a certain strength, and he must send it up if he can.

But there is another consideration beyond those of strength and direction. It is one of the most delightful properties of a curling stone that it "goes with the handle"; that is, turns to right or left as it runs. Here again everything depends upon the ice. In Scotland the curl of a stone is almost a negligible quantity. It may be made to turn a few inches under good circumstances or by means of the turn a stone may often be kept straight against a "lead" in the ice, which would otherwise have caused it to fall away. But it is hardly a practical factor in the game. Much depends on the ice, and much also depends upon the cut of the stones, but generally speaking, the "turn of the handle" is in Canada and Switzerland a matter of quite vital importance. For under certain conditions a stone may not only be made to turn at will, but must turn whether one will or not. If it is delivered with a straight handle it will take up a turn as it runs, and before it reaches the hog will be slowly swinging either to right or left. So it is essential for the player to make up his mind which turn he will play. It will readily be understood what an interest and variety this additional factor lends to the game,

c

and how many new shots are made possible by its use. It is as if one need not approach the tee by the high road, but may slip in by winding byways where from the crampit no opening can be seen in the protecting mass of guards.

The "in-turn" or "in-elbow" causes the stone to swing to the right, and the "out-turn" to the left, or in other words the in-turn is equivalent to an off-break, and the out-turn to a leg-break. The turn is put on to the stone entirely with the wrist just at the moment of delivery. It is wrong, in spite of its name, to attempt to put it on with the elbow.

Even on the keenest ice it is possible to play a perfectly straight shot, if it be played strongly enough, and this is a point on which many of the foreign curlers have still something to learn. They have become so accustomed to the turn that it does not seem to occur to them to play a straight "running" shot, and I have occasionally seen a stone lying open on the tee, which the skip did not attempt to dislodge because there were guards preventing approach from either right or left.

The player, as soon as he has delivered his own stones takes up his position about half-way down the rink, with his broom in hand, and again awaits instructions from his skip. Sweeping is a highly important factor in the game, far more important than the unschooled spectator ever understands. However keen the ice may be, the side that sweeps lustily and intelligently, beginning and stopping at the right moment so as to keep a turning stone straight, or allow a straight stone to turn, is in many cases the side that wins. There is a type of Swiss curler, who likes to gaze at the mountains with his broom under his arm, and assures you that there is nothing on the ice to sweep away. Perhaps to his poor limited vision it may appear so, but one is tempted to point out to him that he will get a better view of the mountains from the verandah of the hotel.

V

THE SKIP

IT is a part of the very essence of the game of curling that the authority of the skip shall be supreme. On him alone rests the entire responsibility of directing the campaign, and except when he is delivering his own stones, he controls the whole play of his side from his stand in the house. In all the world of sport there is surely no more honourable or responsible position than that of a skip who captains a rink of three great curlers. A poet is born and not made, but a long study of curling has led me to the conclusion that a skip must be both born and made. To attain a final perfection it seems to me that he must be steeped in curling. His first acquaintance with the game should date from an early voyage of discovery upon his hands and knees, when he comes upon a stone at either side of the hearth; and he should find a "besom" in the eight-day clock when first his curiosity prompts him to look inside it. He should be capable of playing truant from school in frosty weather to watch the parish matches, and he should not be long content with watching. As soon as he has left the school he should be a regular member of a rink, and after "leading" for some ten years, and playing in other positions for twenty-five or thirty, before he has lost the full strength and mental vigour of his manhood, and with the ripe experience and settled judgment of

THE SKIP

late middle age, the time has come for him to skip a
rink of his own, always provided that he has been
richly endowed with the necessary qualities at the
outset.

He must in the first place have a thorough knowledge
both of his men and their capabilities, and of the stones
they are playing. He must know by long experience
what shot the player of the moment is capable of doing,
and he must know by instinct the moment when that
player is capable of a shot beyond his ordinary powers.
He must judge the pace of the running stone (and no
two pairs of stones behave alike), and he must be
continually adjusting himself to the frequent changes
in the state of the ice. But the chief of his duties is
in the building of the end, and here he has ample
score for his best talents of observation and generalship. For one may curl for a lifetime and see no two
ends exactly the same.

First he will bring up his "lead" either with one
stone on each side of the tee, or, if they must keep
the centre, with one stone covering the other. In
neither case will he bring them too far, for to come to
the tee is merely to give a "rest" to your opponent,
who will stop on the face of your stone, playing it out,
and taking its place. As the end develops he brings
up his shots, and lays his guards, frustrating the
tactics of his opponent and forestalling him wherever
he can. He will never be content with one shot in a
winning position, but will have a second or third in
reserve, lest, his winner being played out, the other
side counts a "big head." Indeed he will be in no
great hurry to have a winner on the tee, until he sees
his position secure from attack. Often he will guard
a dangerous stone of his opponent's and sometimes he
will play it through, though it be not even in the
house, for his thoughts are by no means confined to

the winning shot. He plays always for the strength
of the whole end, and the shots will follow, "as the
night the day." He must take the measure of his
opponents and know what chances he may give them
with impunity, and he must know well his own powers
as a player. In a desperate position he may leave for
his own last stones the delicate and risky shot that he
did not dare to give to Number 3.

Such are the purely technical qualities and attain-
ments of my ideal skip. But all that I have described
is merely the groundwork of his endowments, and will
carry him only so far as the science of curling goes.
And curling is far more than a science. The perfect
skip must not only be capable of absolute concentration
upon the game—all else should melt into oblivion for
the time being—but must display great qualities of
heart and head. He must be a leader of men, both
the brain and the driving power of his side. He must
preserve a perfect equanimity when the tide of battle
is against him, and he must keep his side in good
heart under impending defeat. For curling is "a
slippery game," and the most surprising turns of
fortune may at any moment save the day. He must
have perfect control over his temper, and a perfect
generosity in accepting a wild and wayward shot;
ready, when it fails to do what he wanted, to make it
do something else. And he must maintain a perfect
courtesy in his dealings with the opposing skip. For
the two skips are brought during a match into a close
and interesting relation. They stand side by side in
the house, for hours on end, the one awaiting the
coming stone, the other ready to pounce upon it the
moment it reaches the tee and sweep it out, each of
them conning the situation, and putting forth all his
powers to outwit the other. And through it all they
must be careful not to impede each other's movements

DELICATE AND DAINTY.

AT THE TOP OF A LONG SWING.

21

and to keep up towards one another a friendly and even a sympathetic attitude.

And finally, my skip must not be a silent man, or a man of few words. There is no doubt at all in my mind that the nature of the skip's directions tell greatly in curling. I would have him, in giving directions and in generally addressing his men, genial, eloquent, humorous and voluble. The flow of his discourse should increase with his waning fortunes, and the whole rink should be inspired and kept together by the pith and pertinence of his observations. One such great skip I knew who was so lavish in his expenditure of voice, that by the third day of play (in spite of the friendly eucalyptus lozenge which was never absent from his waistcoat pocket) it would fail him altogether. After that he fell back on signs and whispers. But his players suffered. I was always glad when it so happened that I was drawn against him during the silent period.

VI

THE SINGLE-HANDED GAME

THE " Points," or single-handed game is a sort of by-product of the game of curling. It is a test of cold, scientific accuracy, in which there is no question of generalship, no building of the end, no lusty sweeping, no sudden freaks of fortune, and little of the joy of battle. It comprises certain set shots—all the leading shots in the game—and the winner is he who scores the largest number of points. In each case two points are given for a perfect shot, and one for a shot that is partially successful.

Most clubs devote one day in the season to a single-handed competition. Two rinks are used, and every player plays a pair of stones up and down, thus having four chances at each " point." A diagram is drawn on the ice, showing the position of the objective stones. The problems set are nine in number. The competitor is first called upon to " strike," that is, play out a stone which is lying on the tee. The next shot is " inwicking," which consists in cannoning from one stone to another. He has also to " draw " and to " guard," which require no explanation. The fifth point is " chap and lie," which curious expression means striking a stone in such a manner that one's own stone stops at the point of impact. This is followed by " wick and curl in," which is a cannon off a side stone into the house. " Raising " is number seven. Here one has to strike a stone, belonging to one's own side and lying in front of the house, in such a way as to play it in. "Chipping the winner" follows. The stones are so placed that the one, lying on the tee—which represents an opponent— is partly guarded, and only half of it can be seen from the crampit. The shot consists of passing the guard and striking the winning stone. And finally the player must "draw a port," that is to say, pass between two stones lying close together, into the house.

It is generally recognised that there is no "follow through" in a curling-stone—that is to say, however hard it may be played, if it strikes another stone fairly in the centre it stops dead. I was myself so certain of this fact that when playing last winter on perfect ice at Grindelwald, I was completely amazed and disconcerted by what I could only regard as a phenomenon quite outside of the accepted order of things. I think I would hardly have been more shocked at the sight of water running up hill. For a stone in the game that I was playing deliberately followed through at least two feet, and furthermore stopped on the tee. I tried a number of experimental shots after the game was over, but I could never get the same result. So I was forced to accept the matter as yet another curling mystery, and belonging to that undiscovered country which no curler in one brief life-time can ever hope to explore. I think it is the grandest quality of curling that there is always something new to learn, always something in reserve that baffles analysis. In the dullest and most humdrum game one is never beyond the scope of delightful surprises. As long as one is dealing with such uncertain factors as ice and curling-stones, and the mental and physical powers of man, one cannot hope to gauge with any degree of finality the limit of a moment's possibilities.

The highest attainable score in the points game is seventy-two, and it must be admitted that the records do not seem to approach it very closely. But it is one of the peculiarities of this form of curling that it is by no means so easy as it looks. Shots that one can confidently count upon playing correctly in the course of a game do not seem always to come off under these less inspiring conditions. In drawing and guarding, again, one has not the assistance of the brooms to fall back upon. One is indeed allowed to sweep one's own stone, but it requires a good deal of activity to recover oneself after playing and catch up the running stone before it reaches the hog. Finally, it is a different thing to play at a single stone, lying alone in open ice, from playing to the skip's broom in a crowded house. I fancy that in the latter case the stones lying on either side help to guide the eye.

However that may be, it is a fact that out of a possible score of 72 a total of 25 is generally good enough to win a medal, and in Scotland or Switzerland anything above 30 ranks as very good indeed. Nowhere is the supremacy of Canadian curling more evident than in the points game. Scores of 50 and over have been recorded there. But the present holder of the world's record is a member of the United States' Club of St. Paul's, with the splendid total of 62.

VII

CURLING IN SCOTLAND

THE enthusiasm of the Scottish curler is a long triumph of hope over experience. Year after year clubs must hold their meetings and transact their business, and a vast machinery must be set in motion, collecting subscriptions, arranging cups and bonspiels, making "draws" and printing time-tables of special trains, and in the great majority of cases all this widespread activity comes to naught. An open winter is a national calamity. The record of the last few years alone will show on what poor shreds and patches the interest in curling must subsist. There has not been a real, full-blooded season since the early months of 1895, when play went forward for ten weeks on end. There were two or three weeks of play in '97 and '99, and a brief spell of fine ice in February 1902. But I do not think there has been a fortnight of consecutive curling throughout the country for the last six years. The Grand Match at Carsbreck was last played in 1903, and the International Match between England and Scotland has only been carried out three times since its inauguration in 1895. During the past winter about three days' play on very indifferent ice was probably the average in most districts.

Since ice has become so rare a commodity much has been done in the last ten years in the direction of forming artificial curling rinks, and great ingenuity is now displayed in the art of making a little frost go a long way. There are many concrete rinks, which can be flooded with an inch of water, and are usually frozen solid after the second night of frost. In a changeable season a large number of odd games may be brought off in this way, when deep water is never fit to play on. The latest pattern of artificial curling rink is made of what is known as "Tarmac." It has a perfectly level surface, and the water is simply sprayed on, to the thickness of a penny, so that on any frosty morning a sheet of ice may be obtained in a few minutes. But there has recently been a movement among Glasgow curlers towards freeing themselves altogether from the uncertain favours of Nature, and a glaciarum was opened at Crossmyloof in October 1907, where play has been going forward merrily on manufactured ice. In all these various ways curlers have been labouring to overcome climatic disabilities, and by hook or by crook to keep the game alive. But every one of them knows in his heart of hearts that they are but makeshifts after all, a mere feeble echo of the glories of a bonspiel on the ringing ice of a frozen lake.

It may well be that the many disappointments, the long list of broken hopes, the uncertainty of what the morrow will bring forth, all go to make up the enthusiasm and the zest with which the curler seizes his opportunity when at last it does arrive. For the climate of Scotland is like the little girl of the nursery rhyme. When it is good, it is very, very good. And when it is bad, it is horrid. And it is generally horrid. But even at its worst, when the south-west wind is rolling up great billows of rain, and all the world is moist and grey, a change may come at any moment. The curler wakes one morning to find sharper, cleaner air, and a cloudless sky, with a light breeze from the

On a Dumfriesshire Loch.

north-west. The puddles on the road are already speared over with shafts of ice and the fire is burning frostily. The whole landscape is clear and glittering in the sun, which sets red as the afternoon wears on, and is followed by a glorious night of stars. Before he goes to bed the curler has looked his handles over, and spent an hour by the fireside splicing his broom.

Whether it come in November or in February, there is no ice quite like the first ice. By the third day of the frost, the entire parish has laid down its tools and headed for the meeting-place, and one may hear a mile off the deep roar of the stones, a sound which fires the curler's heart, like the blast of a bugle. It is a sound which belongs to Scotland alone, for a stone runs silently on solid ice, and only gives tongue on deep water. And so the loch, which a week ago lay deserted among the hills, drearily lashed by wind and rain, is now a royal battlefield, where a scene of indescribable hilarity and good humour is going forward to the yells of the victors and the groans of the vanquished.

There are two things besides the climate which militate against the game of curling in Scotland. In the first place it labours beneath a multiplicity of cups and trophies. There is not a word to be said against cups in moderation, but they now entail so heavy a programme, on such a limited supply of ice, that the old parish "spiel," once the backbone of the game, is falling more and more into abeyance. One cannot but regret that these fine old feuds, some of them dating back for generations, should be allowed to die. The other matter which tends to limit interest in the game is the prevalence of one-sided matches. In both the great bonspiels the opposing sides are quite unequally matched. Scotland is much too strong for England, and has always won by a large majority, while in the Grand Match, the South of Scotland has won every encounter for nearly thirty years. There is, it must be added, always the additional interest besides the actual result, which attaches to the rink that wins the cup.

But the Scot's main complaint is simply the want of ice. Given another winter like that of 1894–1895, curling will proclaim with no uncertain voice what a tremendous power it still is in the land.

VIII

CURLING IN SWITZERLAND

THERE is a wide difference between the scene that I have just described and that which is enacted every day throughout the winter season at Davos or St. Moritz. Here the game of curling is lifted out of all vicissitudes of climate, and unaffected by sudden changes in the ice. It is simplified, and made beautiful. Instead of the rough black ice of the Scotch loch, the "board" is like a slab of polished marble, wherein one can see the stone reflected, as if it floated on still water. The rings are marked beneath the surface in coloured chalk, and a body of men, under expert guidance, are at work, morning and evening, polishing, shaving, spraying and flooding the ice. There is a boy with a wooden spoon and a pail of water, who potters about filling up little cracks and rubbing down excrescences. The rink is set in the heart of a glittering picture, with giant peaks in the distance, and vast snowfields, sprinkled over with châlets in the foreground; and the whole is flooded with sunshine from a cloudless sky. The game itself is a delicate, dainty, silent performance, with an absence of effort and an ease and grace in all its movements that has earned for it the name—invented no doubt by some contemptuous Scot—of "drawing-room curling." Here Scotland's "roaring game" has become a game of whispers. The stones glide up the

33

rink as silently as a billiard ball, and the players on their rubber soles move without a sound.

St. Moritz, Grindelwald, and Davos are the three leading Alpine clubs. St. Moritz is the highest curling club, above sea-level, in the world, being situated at an altitude of over six thousand feet. The ice in that intense frost is extremely hard and brittle, and often " borrows" so much that a stone to reach the tee must be played at a broom placed right outside the house to allow for the " handle." St. Moritz generally leads the way in all winter sports, and curling is no exception to the rule. It has held the Jackson Cup—the Swiss championship trophy—ever since it was presented. Grindelwald is also a great curling centre, with a club membership of over a hundred. In both of these clubs, and also at Davos, there are a large number of lady players, who have no difficulty at all on the keen Swiss ice in holding their own, though the game is rather beyond their strength in Scotland.

An annual international bonspiel has been held in Switzerland for the last four winters. It was inaugurated at Kandersteg in 1905 with very happy results. An invading force of over a hundred Scotchmen assembled to do battle for the cup, and the Swiss clubs of the Bernese Oberland were quite unable to withstand their onslaught. Villars, Adelboden. Kandersteg, and Grindelwald went down before them, and for the first two years the cup went home to Scotland. The following year it was won by a Yorkshireman. In 1908 the meeting was held at Celerina, and the St. Moritz curlers were triumphant. On their own ice—Celerina is close to St. Moritz—they may well prove to be invincible. But whether they play under the colours of St. Moritz, of Davos, or of Toronto the vast majority of curlers all the world over are Scotchmen. The game never seems to have really

KANDERSTEG BONSPIEL IN 1906.

35

taken root, without a Scot, and generally a Dumfries-shire Scot, at the back of it. There are many of the younger clubs in Switzerland which seem to me to be suffering from the lack of that Scot. In the newer Alpine resorts, hotel managers very wisely consider a curling rink, and a set of stones a necessary part of their equipment, and the rink is made and the stones set out in symmetrical array at the side of it. But if there be no real curler in the great inrush of winter visitors, to set the ball a-rolling, the matter goes no further. The more playful of the guests after a while will turn their attention with bland inquiry to these strange implements, and in the absence of information will set themselves to invent weird and childlike games with them. I have often thought that if a Scottish labourer were to come up the lane he might drop a silent tear when he saw to what base uses great opportunities may be put.

IX

CURLING IN CANADA

CURLING in Canada is the ultimate development, the *edition de luxe*, the last word. Scotland's country game has come to town, and learned a hundred urban arts and graces. It has lost its rural simplicity, and flourishes as an elaborate product of an ingenious civilisation. Here, in vast covered rinks lighted by electricity and surrounded by a plate-glass gallery, wherein the spectators can have a fine view of the play without having to face the rigours of the frost, the real wizards of the game are gathered together. There are a dozen such covered rinks in Toronto alone. Curling may almost be said to have been transformed into an indoor game, and is chiefly played in the evening after the work of the day is over. It is greatly elaborated in all its details. The ice is treated with much care and ingenuity. The air is admitted by a row of small holes round the rink, just above the ice, and as soon as a sound and level surface is obtained, the process known as "pebbling" is begun. The Canadian is not satisfied with the slight, occasional roughness of the natural ice, and must have a surface that will give an even grip to the stone on any part of the rink. Pebbling is an extremely curious and effective process. It consists of sprinkling the ice with a small jet of boiling water, which is thrown back and forward diagonally, so as to make a diamond pattern. This process is repeated frequently during the season, so that all signs of wear and tear are done away.

Another point in which the Canadians have elaborated the game is in the matter of sweeping. It is a quite amazing thing to see the brooms descend upon a running stone like a tornado and with tremendous expenditure of skill and muscle speed it upon its way. For on Canadian ice there is a new significance in sweeping. It is not only a question of the pace of a stone, but also of the curve that it is taking. This curve may be perceptibly altered, with the result that the stone slips round a guard or finds its way up a port, through the agency of the brooms. The Canadians make a curious claim with regard to sweeping, which Scotch curlers are not always ready to admit, namely that their hurricane methods create a vacuum in front of the stone, and so draw it on. Any one who has seen the effect of a strong wind upon keen ice will be inclined to acknowledge the possibility of this.

In the year 1902 a team of Scotch curlers visited Canada, and played a long series of matches against the native clubs. For many of them it was a great voyage of discovery, but they found themselves, generally speaking, quite outplayed. The Canadian curler is a product of the Canadian climate, and cannot be produced north of the Tweed.

The great Bonspiel at Winnipeg is the contest of the giants. Picked champions from all over Canada, some of whom have travelled 1500 miles to attend, assemble in their hundreds. The meeting assumes the proportions of a festival, and the city is taxed to the utmost to accommodate the guests. Curling reports, with glaring headlines, fill the newspapers, curling sermons are preached in the churches, and day and night, without a breathing-space, the struggle is maintained for twelve or fourteen days.

I cannot perhaps do better than quote the last words—as reported—of a dying Scotch curler : "Let me be buried in Winnipeg."

X

MEMORIES OF THE ICE

In the storehouse of one's curling memories there are
many strange and vivid scenes. It is a brilliant day
at Grindelwald, late in February. The sun tempera-
ture upon the rink is 92 degrees, and yet the ice is
perfectly keen and true, and has no more than a slight
" coom," as we say in Scotland, on its surface. I
stroll about the rink coatless and in a panama hat,
and as the sun swings low in the west must deliver my
stone along a dazzling track of golden light to the spot
where the skip is standing like a figure on a shining
pedestal.

It is five o'clock on a March morning in Scotland.
A sudden snap of frost has tempted me to snatch yet
another game before the season closes, but I know that
if I wait till the sun is up the ice will waste away in a
few hours. As it is, there are 22° of frost when the
game begins in the twilight, and I come in to breakfast
with the satisfaction of eighteen ends behind me
played on a perfect board, and with the appetite of a
boa-constrictor.

Or, again, it is the evening of Christmas day, and I
have been watching the artificial rink since early morning, and found the ice making very slowly. But at
this festive season we are in no mood to be baffled by
want of daylight, and when the frost sets in keen in
the afternoon, torches and bicycle lamps are requisi-

tioned, and the rings marked out. The game begins about 9 P.M. and goes on far into the night. It is a strange romantic scene, and the state of things generally is perhaps not conductive to the best curling, for in addition to the fitful light and the black shadows cast across the ice, a heavy fall of snow begins about the fifth end, and it is lying to the depth of several inches before the proceedings terminate. And yet it is a great and memorable victory, won, as a curling match should always be, by the last stone.

Or it is a bonspiel on a Dumfriesshire loch, where eight local clubs are met in the throes of conflict. A whole sheep, slaughtered for the occasion, has gone into the making of the Hot Pot, with which the players pause to regale themselves at half-time. There are thirty-two rinks competing, covering some two or three acres of ice. A litter of carts, baskets and overcoats, spreads along the bank. This is the outstanding day of the winter season, the climax of the local curler's achievements. But while the Hot Pot is still being handed round, a horrid searching wind comes sweeping down the valley from the north-east, and in an hour or two the cold, clammy hand of the thaw has snuffed out these rare delights, for the umpire has declared the ice unsafe. It must not be supposed that a mere deterioration in the ice would have caused a suspension of hostilities, so long as it was strong enough to bear the weight of men and stones. I have played many grand games in heavy rain, when the stone ran through half an inch of water forming as it went a wave like that made by the bow of a vessel. Sometimes by the last end the ice is swaying, bending, and cracking to right and left, and a cunning sweeper may turn the course of a stone by throwing his weight to this or that side of it. Where the stones are gathered together in the house there is a visible dip in the surface, and the skip dare not take his place among them, but stands afar off, directing gingerly. Almost before the last stone has come to rest there is a mad stampede for the bank, every man saving his stones as best he may, and glad to be well out of it without a ducking.

But one has many more technical, and not less precious memories, of great ends that one has played, great shots that one has seen—of moments of super-human prowess, and of those rare days that come to every good curler, when a sense of power descends upon him, and for once he knows that he can do what he is told. I knew one, who kept a small rink drawn to scale in his study, and by placing coins upon it to represent the stones, would play over again in the evening the game that had occupied him during the day. He would reconstruct for my benefit almost every end in order, and I would often leave him with his diagram before him lost in thought, pondering upon the eternal question of what might have been if only——.

Of the outstanding shots that one remembers, it is not, I think, the heroic running shot, that comes up like a lyddite shell, and changes the whole complexion of the house, by assault and battery, that one prizes most. It is rather the canny, insinuating draw, that has crept sweetly up a long and narrow port, skirting a dozen dangers on its way, and spoiled the chances of the enemy by sidling finally to the tee.

Curling is surely something more than a recreation. It is a Cause, a Brotherhood. I have no space to tell of the mysteries of the Curling Court, and its ceremony of " initiation," or of the traditional grip of the hand exchanged by the Inner Circle wherever they may meet. But something I must say of the curling phraseology. The game is restricted to no mere technical terms, or professional slang. It has a vocabulary, one might almost say a language, of its own, a vocabulary infinitely rich in happy phrases, replete with humour, and often touched with poetry. For there is no limit to the flights of fancy, or bursts of eloquence, with which a skip, now commanding, now advising, now gently pleading, will address his player on the crampit. In his sterner mood he will point to a winning stone that lies behind a bank of guards. "Make a road to that," he will command. But in the next moment he may be melted to tenderness. "Davie," he will cry, with a tear in his voice, "for the love o' the game, gie me a guaird." Again he will try to wheedle a shot out of the player by coaxing him with soft words. "Just cuddle in to grannie's wing," or "Creep up and lie on the bosom of the winner." When he asks for a "Shaughlin' guaird," it is probable that he could not himself explain what he means by the expression, but the player will *feel*, though he could not tell, what is wanted. "Come snooflin' up the port, and crack an egg on that yin," is also a much simpler direction than it appears to be. At times it is a sudden shock of disappointment that gives him voice. When there is a lead in the ice which falls away to the side, and a vital stone despatched with some high mission slips down into this fatal course, he will straighten himself suddenly, with despair writ large upon his countenance. "Eh, man," he will cry, "ye're doon cuddy lane!"

But the heart of curling is in the note of generosity which pervades it, and in the tradition that all men are equal on the ice. Here, as in no other game, meet men of all ages, all social positions, and every walk of life. The one absorbing passion is supreme. In every parish curling keeps an open

door. The note of generosity is nowhere more in
evidence than in the general desire to make the best
of things, and the general unwillingness to blame,
which is also a tradition. The skip will acclaim your
good shot with a yell of triumph, but he will not
admit that there is anything wrong with your bad
one. He is ready to blame the ice, the stone, the
wind, the sun or anything but the hand that played
the shot. You have come roaring up the rink and
shattered his well-built end, scattering his guards or
chipping out his winner. But he will look at you
more in sorrow than in anger, and bravely tell once
more the well-worn lie. "There's no hairm done,
Davie, my man," he will say. "We're a' the better
o' that."

Printed in the USA
CPSIA information can be obtained
at www.ICGtesting.com
LVHW090441251123
764788LV00003B/170